ALL OF IT

(THE ARRANGING OF
A DESTINY. I
ELUDE
BY ACTS OF
MELLOWEST
VENGEANCE

TO ISOLATE
THE POEM
SO THAT
ITS HUMANITY
OF WEEPING ONCE
MORE CAN BE HEARD)

JAH 94

IN PLACE OF ME

Poems by Doreen Stock

IN PLACE OF ME

Poems by Doreen Stock

Selected and with an Introduction
by Jack Hirschman

For Love
For memory / Bob
For Susie & Bob
n—♡ as ever,
Dorey
8/15

Mine Gallery Editions

MINE

In Place of Me

ISBN 978-0-9909203-0-4 (hardcover)
ISBN 978-0-9909203-1-1 (paperback)
ISBN 978-0-9909203-2-8 (EPUB)
ISBN 978-0-9909203-3-5 (MOBI)

Cover design by Amy Drozd, Mine Gallery Editions, from a Kaballah Broadside created by Jack Hirschman with an alphabet of Hebrew letters purchased in a London Garage Sale, 1969.

For more information contact: doreen@doreenstock.com

for Revelation
for Revolution
for Justice
for Jack

ACKNOWLEDGMENTS

I wish to extend thanks to Jack Hirschman for his kind attention to the entire body of my work for ten years past in order to create this collection, and to the editors of the magazines in which the following poems have previously appeared:

Nashim: "Oasis and Desire."

Poetry Greece: "In the Old Mosque," "The Sweetness Problem."

Haight Ashbury Literary Journal: "Kaballah."

Tambourine: "Wings of Another Era."

The Redwood Coast Review: "I Was Swimming."

The Third Tiger, Travel Journal, published by Nomad Travels: "Tigers."

The Marin Poetry Center Anthologies:
Volume Five, 2002: "We Plant Children," "I Was Swimming," "Eating Pizza with the Jews," "Torture."
Volume Nine, 2006: "Redeemed Criminal Being Executed."
Volume Ten, 2007: "Blue Tango #1."
Volume Eleven, 2008: "For Two Schoolgirls/Logar Province, Afghanistan," "Reading Etgar Keret in Café Lo Cubano."
Volume Twelve, 2009: "To An Oud," "Last Tango in Buenos Aires," "For You in the Dark with a Coke," "For Hannah Crossing into Snow."

Washington Square Review, summer '09: "A Camel is Kneeling on the Far Side of the World."

Revolutionary Poets Brigade, Vol. I: "Redeemed Criminal Being Executed."

California Quarterly, Vol. 37, no. 1: "The Order of Words."

CONTENTS

BIRD WITH BLUE (MY) EYES/ POEMS OF SAFED   2002

ANTIGONE AND APHRODITE/POEMS OF CORFU 2001

THE GOD OF WAR   2001

THE DIG AT EIN GEDI   2001

TAMBOURINE   2000

POEMS OF MY SPANISH SUMMER   1998

PAINTING IN THE DARK   1998

DOREEN STOCK: AN INTRODUCTION

A few years ago, at a poetry reading at the Red Poppy Cafe (now the Red Poppy Art House) in the Mission District of San Francisco, I happened to see my old friend Doreen Stock again. I recall that it had been a number of years since we'd last met—she lived in Stinson Beach and, during those same years, I'd been traveling a lot in Europe, at times up to five months out of a year—but in a way she was never too far away, and for a special reason: Doreen was the poet I knew in the '70s—when I started translating from Russian, and then actually started writing poems in Russian—who also was translating from Russian. She especially loved the poems of Anna Akhmatova and Marina Tsvetaeva. She also worked at times in a collective of translators that published a multilingual magazine of revolutionary poetry, *Compages*. And she had a small press of her own, and had published translations from Russian, of a little-known but extraordinary émigré poet, Natasha Belyaeva, in a book called *Hunger*, which I had translated.

As for her own poems, in the '70s and '80s she'd come over the Golden Gate Bridge from Mill Valley, where she lived before her divorce and removal to Stinson Beach. She was raising three children, but she'd participate in North Beach readings and often one saw her at the Intersection on Union Street.

At times, maybe once a year, she'd mail me a new book of poems she'd written. She'd obviously printed it herself—there'd be 25 or 50 copies—and organized a cover drawing or collage. The book was for friends or poets she admired, here and abroad. She wrote I thought well, sensitively, with lyrical sincerity in her love poems, though there was an aura about her work of a deliberateness I couldn't fathom. Like myself, she overused the word "forever" in her work—usually as a kind of emphatic romanticism, like the way we'd send each other's letters or postcards through the years signed: *Vsyegda* (Always). But by and large, and exclusive of the Russian dimension, I'd have to admit that I hadn't given too much thought to Doreen's poetry.

That is, until a couple of years ago, when it happened rather all at once that I was given the insight by a poem of hers to realize that for a long time I had not fully recognized the importance of the poetry of Doreen Stock.

That poem, "Redeemed Criminal Being Executed: San Quentin, December 13, 2005, for Tookie Williams," is the one that sent me back reading through all the chapbooks that Doreen had sent me through the years. It made me realize that it wasn't just a sincerity and lyricism of feeling that had been the substance of her poetry; she has developed through the years a mastery of a form of what I call projective heart-speak. Such a nomination redounds, on the one hand, to some of the principles enunciated in Charles Olson's by now modern classical "Projective Verse" essay. Olson sought to not merely "open" modern poetry (which already had occurred, i.e., Whitman, William Carlos Williams, etc.) but, within a projective leap of language, to manifest the unique way a particular poet thinks and feels using in this instrument we have called the American language.

Like a bolt out of the blue, I realized that Stock had managed to develop the three aspects of projective that are essential to the poem: the first of course is the heart-speak, the facing of the *whatness* that is being felt as the object of one's being called to write the very poem, the object that is in fact demanding the leap of language; the second aspect of her particular mastery is that she has remained faithful to that tension between poetry and prosody, a tension that has been the result of all the invasions of technology on human sensibility, with the result that her mind and inner-speech are at home in the world of the verbal montage of images (here, her translation experience also plays a part), which leads to the third aspect of her style: she has become an expert at controlling the speeds of her poems, and this auto-motive aspect of poetic expression is not something to be scoffed at—not simply because most people's minds spend an hour or two a day in motion in cars, but because that motion and the inner workings of mind and heart have played important parts in shaping or reshaping our poetry.

In the poem for Tookie Williams, an African-American who allegedly committed murder some 30 years ago and had become a renowned writer of children's books in prison, Doreen Stock focuses on the day of his execution. She is not with the thousands who gather at the gates of San Quentin in protest; she's in fact swimming in a lighted pool. But her identity with his agony is so powerful that she is in fact with Williams in the death chamber. Here, in part:

> *the lifeguard sitting above me*
> *on his solitary perch hooded against the December*
> *chill his eyes on me I breathed in swam lap*
> *after lap in a black swimsuit through the cold night*
> *water me breathing in and out as you did, in and*
> *out breathing in your life and letting it go they say*
> *you waved the presence of clergy presenting yourself*
> *calmly, just you and the poison like so much water to*
> *heave your soul through until it passed between the*
> *great lights and the lesser lights and swam its final*
> *laps then dripping and shivering let your shuddering*
> *body go crossing over my name, the name of any*
> *ordinary California citizen that didn't elect this governor*
> *or choose this method or sanction this fate for you*

I focus on this poem for it was the occasion of my seeing Stock's work in another light. Until this poem I had been aware of her lyrical praise/poems—songs, really—of love and nourishment, poems of the heart spoken for the most part directly and warmly. In the poem for Williams, a deeper identity was taking place—at least linguistically—so that the poem is not so rooted in sentiment as it is in a transference of the rage of protest to an in-sighting of the being of self and other as one and the same, though in different spaces.

She would, three years later, write another brilliant poem, about Cho, the young man who went berserk and killed a number of his classmates. But it was the poem on Tookie Williams that first gave me the idea of putting a book of this wonderful poet's work together, selecting poems from each of the more than a dozen chapbooks that she'd given me through the years, and finishing the selection with many of the poems from her latest offering, *Just Like in the Song of Songs*, which is a book of prose poems. The prose poem is perhaps an apt title for the mode in which Doreen is "the most 'me'," but whereas traditional prose poems cover the whole line of space on a page, she has so fused the prose modality with the verse line, achieving the ability to tap in on, as it were, an interweaving inner discourse so that the ebb and flow of her lines create points of lyrical epiphany and insight manifested as nothing other than what poetry itself does, revealing with great consistency and brilliance how Stock has taken hold of the instinctual essence of the projective modes of creation in as natural a manner as anyone writing, and made it the core of her technique.

The title of this book is Doreen's. I think it's a perfect title, *In Place of Me*. It evokes exactly this woman, who was born in St. Paul, Minnesota, in 1942, was a student in California universities in the '60s, and has been as naturally modest and yet intensely dedicated to the art of poetry as any woman of substance. The title of course implies her not-being in place, but *this (the poetry)* is what is here in her stead—that is, the essence of her heart and soul.

I'm honored to have been able in any way to help bring these beautiful poems of love and social and political awareness to more than just a chapbook audience. The selection of poems is placed chronologically in reverse, beginning with 2008, though the book will end with work from the 2009 *Just Like in the Song of Songs* chapbook.

Jack Hirschman
San Francisco
2009

RIDING THE LOTUS
2008

WHEN I AM JUNK

When I am junk
a headlight flung into a tree or

a right ankle (the one pinned,
re-broken, plated and in a third operation
to have the metal removed, restored
to its hiking boot after the divorce) spun
toward the gutter like a bowling pin
targeted in the darkest of alleys

lips blown away from their last
kiss, arms torn from their last hug, a
torso steeped in journals of neoclassical
rubbish, a heart having thumped its last
irregular line,

love my words, and when they are gone
love the gesture of my left hand before it held
the pen that wrote them as it was placed on my
breast where the poems began their ardent
journey toward my throat, love this impulse
in yourself and let poetry rise into whatever
new day you may find yourself opening
toward after your night of dreams.

12/30/07

I AND THOU

Eyes forward as if staring at the same target on an invisible dartboard
you two are caught in profile by our photographer from the Kremlin
photo pool crisp white shirts dark Putin and Ahmadinejad shoulders.
What are you staring at? Could it be the two others facing you directly?
The journalist Politkovskaya, the human rights lawyer Ebadi, both
women, one alive in Tehran, but on a hit list, one already shot dead on
the front steps of her Moscow apartment…

Today you are condemning the use of force in the area of the Caspian
Sea as in your private circus high-wire act you pose here before flipping
to divest yourselves of the most brilliant women in your time and place.

Shh, Gentlemen, it is being whispered that there are unseen beings you
can't even classify, Leviathan Feminine Caspian forces defying
all nationhood and gravity, lurching toward you, under the giant
waves troubling that inland sea that lies between you, big enough to
assassinate all time.

PARIS CHANGING

for Kaaren

Though kissed by a reverent sun
the truth is this city can't capture
its own royal beauty. Trees disappear
from its parks and the marbles pose
a little less gracefully for the lack
of greening around them

The same streets still do intersect
mysterious corners for the rendezvous
of certain charmed walls, the grasses

in the Luxembourg gardens suffer periodic
ruin as the petals on seasonal blooms
spaded in by the gardeners of Paris curl
and fade. White and serene among them
stands George Sand, she's been through
a lot lately, and the rain, hail, snow ravage
her face, try to sabotage her waistcoat buttons…
As well she knew even the City of Light depends
on the eye for its effects and so you were
changing Paris, my friend, when you cancelled
your flight, subtracting yourself from its walkways.
Something went out of the Eiffel Tower that day,
the Seine darkened under its bridges and Paris
missed you or what you in your black St. John knits
and intelligent gaze would have added to its splendors.

For want of the shades of your hair, your scent
meandering toward a stone interior, Paris lost
a little patina last autumn and stands there
patient as the ages awaiting its eternal return
within you.

ON THE DUMPING OF ROADKILL

The first stanza of this poem
comes from a TV newscast exploring
the plight of veterans returning
from the wars in Iraq and Afghanistan:
¼ of all homeless persons in America
are my soldiers.

The second stanza of this poem
originates in a small local newspaper
article about the dumping
of roadkill in an unauthorized site,
Rodeo Drive, just around the corner
from my new digs, citing the number
of deer skeletons in particular.

The third stanza of this poem tries mightily to create
a connection between stanzas one and two but fails
on a metaphorical level the best I can do being to report a strange
oppressive depressiveness every day as I rise out of my bed parked just
under the freeway north of said dumping site.

The fourth stanza of the poem is reduced to
three words, the best I can do being to articulate them
as if out of a sacred bone caught in the center of my broken neck my
tongue drying out as the traffic whizzes past: Cars… Oil… Death…

Veterans Day, 2007

YOU STAND IN SNOW

Beyond icicles that pierce
the blue air

where distances
ring like the sound we hear
when someone is dying

you stand in snow
so far and deep
the flakes sifting
past your eyelids
and sinking into
the crissy-cross microscopic
chaos of your beard
quieting the evergreens
piling up on their needled
arms

the smell of cold clearing
your mind to turn its little
cartwheels back where the
snow angels have waved
their padded arms to make
the wings you needed to fly
away from me. Lying on your
back little boy could you ever imagine
that the man standing here so tall
and strange in his woolen watch cap
and casting a shadow could ever be you?

THE ORDER OF WORDS

We'd been looking at masks from Africa
that day as they sat in cases of glass grinning
with their small pointed teeth, dark, oily, gleaming,
released from their last funeral dances
by a whole lot of cash changing hands.

And the last object we admired in the museum
was a coffin handmade by an artist of coffins,
its lid hinged, and, we were assured,
possessing a plush interior.

You were wearing a coat the color of fire; we had
the small round black table between us as I recall
and before us a sculpture garden in autumn, trees
spread out on the edge of the great park.

It was November, my jasmine tea steaming, still.
We conversed about Africa, children, death and money,
in just that order, Africa, children, death, and money.

ON THE EDGE OF THAT BLADE

Tonight the Democratic Party debates, broadcasting live from Las Vegas that gambling and fantasy capital of the world also fastest growing American city with the most foreign taxicab drivers, like the one in Salman Rushdie's novel who foretells 9/11. We will watch our countrymen and one countrywoman skate on thin ice over the disappearing middle class, health, and wealth and of how we can shrink wrap the helicopters in Iraq, COD them, bring them home before they attack Iran while they are still needed to pluck our war dead from the fields to be processed by Army chaplains who send them home under the American flag. A single *Wall Street Journal* reporter is watching the candidates apply their TV makeup, tweak their collars, and prepare to speak out to us where we all stand together on the edge of that blade that silenced Daniel Pearl.

READING ETGAR KERET IN CAFÉ LO CUBANO

Two transparent beers
at the edge of the infrared
counter two male elbows
planted next to them
the Gypsy Kings pulsing
through the earlobes
of twenty-five or so patrons
6:30 pm and I call my sweetie
tell him I wish he were here
to read "The Nimrod Flipout,"
title story of Etgar Keret's
collection (who's speaking tonight
at the JCC) when in from California
Street boogies a dusty black
jacket really dirty jeans beneath
it frayed over the tops of sockless
shoes. The gentleman rolls his
eyes at the waitress who frosts
him and unconcerned he dances
up to the water with lemon floating in it
pours some into the paper cup
wrapped with lavender flowers
and takes us all in. At this point
because I've lived in Tel Aviv
a trickle
of leftover cultural panic surfaces
into my throat and I decide that it's been
a good life and if we do all explode this
instant at least I called my sweetie this thought
lasting as he looks from face to face to face to
face and at last bops on out of the door
of the translucent café…

FALLING WITH MOTHER

Swimming being our thing we totter once more over the uncut grass
aluminum walker folded cornered leaving only
the purple cane in your right hand my hand grasping your left, your elbow
bent into the crook of mine in our uneven pilgrimage over the small road the
mail comes in on passing the lemon tree which bonks me on the head the
creaking white iron gate opening outward quite a trick getting you
through it letting it bang shut behind. Our mind's eye having drawn us
into the sunny liquid aqua rectangle we sink and spread euphoric the cool
kissing of shoulders prime consoler for losses our dead loves who swim in
the aching of time

On our way back your black beach shoes squishing squeaking over the
same turf I trip on a paving stone we flop down two overgrown fishes
hauled up onto cement by that big guy in the sky who could have with one
jerk ended either one of us if you believe in that sort of thing but instead
falling with you turns out to be a gentler thing heads cocked toward one
another on the green plastic patio grass where we could still see each
other, talk to one another, decide, what to do, what to do next...

THE NEW YEAR CREEPS IN ON LITTLE POSSUM FEET

Walnut halves buried in the scorched top
of my honey cake this year like lost brain functions
I pull away brown paper bag from glass pan
peel it off the bottom of my baked honey orange
rind flour oil and egg, toss it into the garbage,
sleep the uneasy sleep of one who will soon leave
this seaside palace for an inland apartment while two
eyes on either side of a pink snout engineer the gooky gray lid and among
delectables of watermelon rind and eggshells an old honey container and
other marvels (this is choice, not destiny operating) no it is not the hand of
God but the possum's tiny teeth and quivering nostrils that seize the baked
brown paper morsels, haul them out onto splintered wood fence top and
try to extricate the crumbs leaving this collage: scraps of what's left of the
multiple sweetnesses as the old year, the other hours and years here
dwindle down to the trash to be collected the day after I must truck myself
away…

FOR TWO SCHOOLGIRLS/LOGAR PROVINCE, AFGHANISTAN

For the red carnations
that once were your throats

For the red carnations
that opened all at once
on your young backs

For the red carnations
that flowered through
your hearts

For the purple silence
of your lips
the amethyst bruises
under your eyelids
the dawn lit tears
of the schoolyard little people
who watched you fall in the brown
wheat and your killers vanish

For the carnations that once were
your voices

And the jeweled eyes that only
wanted to read that chalkboard
thick with dust wordless black
space that hangs beyond
you erasing the future of a land
called Afghanistan

For the red carnations
all of them, blooming into
the oblivion of your shattered
smiles.

6/07

CHO

"We do not know if these occurrences are the beginning of
something new—the 'new example,' or the death pangs of a
faculty that mankind is about to lose."
Hannah Arendt, *On Violence*

Like the two eyes
of the deer that
charged my Infiniti
last night on the mountain
not caring that my brights
were on from his narrow
rock ledge I was society's
mistake an engine in his
path thrown upon him as he
crashed against me
somersaulted
over me
and stunned bounced back
up, turned, stared at
my white car body before
crashing down the canyon
to lie there this morning
a being expiring from excess
the sacred world dying
everywhere around him
only alien blackness
because he couldn't see…

*

"You were lucky," said Sal
behind the desk at the auto body.
"If he had broken your windshield
he would have panicked and bitten you
all up; I've seen this, it's not a pretty
sight." And all day in the strange black
mobster car from the rental agency listening
to the details from Virginia Tech wobbling
over familiar landscapes coming unglued
from within until sunset, such pain when I pass
through the night threshold and sense the new trees
springing up along the same mountain road,
thirty-four, one for each student and teacher,
the thirty-fifth for their killer…

*

CNN interviews the gun salesman
his green plaid shirt tucked in
"We ran the check," he maintains, absolving
himself from the carnage.

Carnage is not a word for a poem,
but that's where we are the flag
at half mast over the large University
and "WE ARE VIRGINIA TECH, WE WILL BE VIRGINIA TECH"
a poet as cheerleader at the graduation ceremonies
and Cho's relatives in Korea being interviewed
about his childhood something wrong from the start
they say that something careening headlong into the
classrooms guns blazing

Cho Bam Cho Bam Cho.

4/19/07

CUTTING THE ELEPHANT IN HALF
2007

DIDN'T KNOW WE WOULD GET SO FUNDAMENTAL

Didn't know we would get
so fundamental that day
when I decked you out
for Purim in lipstick and old
scarves so we would look like Esther
the Queen or Vashti the feminist heroine
all of a sudden didn't know I would
look at this photo now and think about
how little I want a harem for anyone

Didn't know we would get
so fundamental and I would
look at this now and think
even then my little boy did not want to
play at tyrant or hero didn't know
we would split out this way two
of you not speaking because one of you
has all the answers the rest of us none
Didn't know we would get so
fundamental that who we married or
didn't marry would make or break
the connection between us as we hugged
each other and you were my three little
loves grinning out at the camera in Shu
Shu Shushan long ago, Persia it was that's
where the short story began, gallows there, too,
and a public hanging didn't know we would
get so Saddam Shiite and Sunni so push the Jews
into the sea again, didn't know then how that
story just goes on and on...

I THOUGHT YOU *WERE* A CAT

I tell the guy, "I dreamt you were offering me a dish of cat food," and begin to laugh in that edgy half hurt way of someone who knows this love story is not going well.

"Cats are emotionally independent," he replies, and I laugh even more bang a few cupboard doors so maybe a glass will fall out and shatter on the floor. They do this at weddings so that even in the moment of greatest joy a bride and groom will remember how fragile love is. I resist the urge to say, "I'm not a cat, I'm a woman," not wanting to state the obvious, but he asks me mischievously if I always bang the cupboard doors like this.

"Sure," I think I'll say, "Always, that's me in the kitchen, I'm just a one-man band!"

But instead I paint the entire kitchen blue.

BLUE TANGO #1

We lit three menorahs the last
night of Hanukkah exchanged
a long kiss in the multiple flames

We tried the American tango, starting in
the blue kitchen with tall ivory candles turning
against the black window glass weaving
around the couch and the seven chairs
crossing over our doubts with pointed steps
and an open embrace how we danced stumbling
past the words building up between us your right
elbow raised high the fingers of my left hand pointing
down against the bulge in your corduroy sleeve

I taught you to let me lunge forward full well knowing
that you could push me back at any second all
your old men all my old women goading us on with their
pointed beards, their underwear of plum-colored satin.
As they were dying in Baghdad we danced suiciding in
Afghanistan danced in Africa burying tiny bodies in
shrouds like the pale fish we forked out of crisp
parchment for our holiday meal.

I dipped into your dark eyes, the worlds spun
and those who had gone before us were roused,
raised themselves painfully up from our tangled limbs
longing to just sip and dine and dancing disrobe
one more time before the night of cold stars and
the tipping moon could descend upon them.

UR EYES MOVING OVER A BED OF RUSHES

Your eyes washed with light of the late day sky
tips of young evergreen and fern fringing them
flashing in silence after our theft of a bed
from the deer in their season

Your eyes ringed with bravery, sorrow, the brown
rainbow gaze stopping all questions brimming with
peace and joy beaming their quiet intelligence
in small tracings as they brush over my face
painting it into that green streaked place

Your eyes moving over a bed of rushes
Your eyes capturing the space the rank
mysteries of a small farm pond beneath us
sealing grace where the wild deer slept
and woke parted the thicket and bounded
inward toward those meadows we only see
in dreams.

ISABELLA

You burp and sleep
little queen
and bring us a taste
of bliss and milk
on your blue wings

I HESITATE

for Fred Kirschner

"I hesitate

I hesitate and this

I hesitate and this doesn't mean

I hesitate and this doesn't mean
that I

I hesitate and this doesn't meant
that I've forgotten

I hesitate and this doesn't mean
that I've forgotten
I know

I hesitate and this doesn't mean
that I've forgotten
I know this story

I hesitate and this doesn't mean
that I've forgotten
I know this story from beginning
to end

I hesitate and this doesn't
mean
       Buchenwald.
       This story
       Buchenwald

This story from beginning
Buchenwald
Buchenwald
This story from beginning
to end, but
            Buchenwald
            Buchenwald
            I don't want to emphasize
      Buchenwald
      Buchenwald
      Buchenwald
      Buchenwald
      Buchenwald
      Buchenwald
        the cruelty..."

We had to sit at the back of the class, our parents said it couldn't get worse Buchenwald Buchenwald but it Buchenwald did.

There was a fence Buchenwald if someone was strolling too close Buchenwald to it people would pull you back.

Buchenwald perhaps a crow flew over the gate Buchenwald the day your name was called Buchenwald and telegraphed to the other crows above Buchenwald as you were freed.

        "Brown eyes"

    said the crow to the other
    crows and cawed Buchenwald Buchenwald
    "brown eyes is alive out of Buchenwald" cawed
    the crow to the others, crows I mean, the day you
    walked out of there Buchenwald "we lost everything
    but our skin and bones" you reported
        freed.

NIC

I wish you could have seen him
on the third day of October come
down to the sea's edge to make
you a cake.

Big! The size of a car tire at least
and three times as high with a
pyramid of sand on the tip.

He bought you two dozen red roses
this year, plus four puffy sunflower-mums
and four pink lilies, the kind with the red
splotches inside. The back of his neck

to the silver-dazzled water he bent
over to decorate his gift with all
of those blossoms and topped
the whole thing with a bottle cap and one

shiny penny. Then must have taken
one of the cut rose stems to print
his message in the sand:
     HAPPY BIRTHDAY
     MOM. I LOVE YOU.
          NIC

Tell me, did you name him NIC, without
a K at the end? He was nowhere in sight
and the tide was coming in.

All this I must write so you'll know
when the flowers arrive who they
are from and that he never forgets.

PARADISE NOW

There are those among us
who blow themselves up
there are those among us
who blow themselves up
there are those among us
who blow themselves up
there are those among us
who blow themselves up
there are those among us
who blow themselves up
among us there are those
who blow themselves up
among us there are those
who blow themselves up
among us there are those
who blow themselves up
among us those who blow
themselves up are among
us those who blow themselves
up are among us those who blow
themselves up There are those
among us who blow themselves
up

RABBI LEAVING AN EXECUTION
SAN QUENTIN, JAN. '06

for Michael Lezak

Sometime past midnight
he turned, not knowing
(none of us knew) if the old
blind inmate who had once
ordered his son's girlfriend
killed for witnessing a robbery
had yet perished at our hands
while the Native Americans
finished their drumming, their
measured cries lingering
in the dark

and walked past the woman holding a candle the youth
costumed in gallows black the young socialista with her
nose ring glittering in the night the giant puppet
of Mahatma Gandhi in a varnished white paper robe

and stepped slowly one white running shoe after the other a black and
white prayer shawl wound around his warm jacket made his way toward
the police as generators whirred harshly and a helicopter chopped the
black and brass sky...

This Rabbi often whispers, "Prick up your ears," so I am
listening as he leaves the pageant we have become to find
the car he parked along the waters of the Richmond Bay
electric jewelry lining its bridge at night I can almost hear

him turn on the ignition, pull away like a prayer that can't
find its way out of this place of crime and counter-killing
but needs to go home and stare down at the heads of the
sleeping children before it can just get off the ground,
let alone fly...

ERIC AND ROSY

ERIC and ROSY
live on a wall

the high winds
skim their letters
spray painted and dried
by the moon

their love is tried
by rain and snow
and when they are lonely

their mute white forms flash
across the *Allée Verte*
to MIKO in silver
and MARILOU and SEMILOU
in black and rose...

ERIC and ROSY
live on a wall
in the *Allée Verte*

and wish for money
and wish to kiss

COLORING THE FACE OF LOVE
2006

REDEEMED CRIMINAL BEING EXECUTED SAN QUENTIN, DECEMBER 13, 2005

for Tookie Williams

Let's say you really did kill four people in the haze
of gang violence 28 years ago in LA...and as the
thousands gather at the prison gates tonight you
are executed by lethal injection in my name, I, I'm
the one who didn't come to watch the one who swam
under that night air in the lit and steaming pool the
bright spotlights lining it and in the dark, where I
couldn't see him the lifeguard sitting above me
on his solitary perch hooded against the December
chill his eyes on me as I breathed in swam lap
after lap in a black swimsuit through the cold night
water me breathing in and out as you did, in and
out breathing in your life and letting it go they say
you waved the presence of clergy presenting yourself
calmly, just you and the poison like so much water to
heave your soul through until it passed between the
great lights and the lesser lights and swam its final
laps then dripping and shivering let your shuddering
body go crossing over my name, the name of any
ordinary California citizen that didn't elect this governor
or choose this method or sanction this fate for you
redeemed or not, criminal or not, my name scrawled on
the petition saying simply not me, do not kill him because
of me so that in the end your death had to pass over my
name with its dark ambiguous wing...

Tell me something, if I re-titled this poem "Woman Drowns
While Lifeguard Looks On" would it come any closer to
what you actually experience on this your last night on
earth...or will you be coming back for more?

BEAUTY

for Billy Amitin

My cousin sits in a chair
with his new-grown hair
the color of cobwebs
in sun.

His laugh is triumphant.
Pity? He will have none
of it. He skates on each
second and turns on the
ice.

Courage? He sit down to
breakfast with a star
in each eye.

He has learned to rise
from wet sheets to attack
the real, and to add and
subtract time
instead of money.
The life he has made sparkles
before him and he looks with
joy at all he has created.

Perhaps today he is wearing
a yellow shirt.

I like him in yellow.

And he smiles equally
on grass and eternity
both of whom he has made
his closest friends.

BROWN RABBI, DANCING

for Stacy Friedman

Her slim form dressed
in brown gauze
brown velvet, her
blue eyes intense
and were this a film
review I would add
smoldering
under a cloud of blond
waves and curls my rabbi
is dancing in dream
time connecting in earthtoned
movements the living
and the dead

We know the soul
is ecstatic she takes
three steps toward the
gate then twirls away
mothlike she enters
a doorway composed
of flame then flies
back out.

A brown moth
wings fringed with tiny
feathers landed
on my Hanukkah menorah
this year, the seventh night,
the seven candles creating
their higher dimensions
and I whisked it away
before it should burn
but ah, the tones of your
voice, whatever am I to do
with these?

POEM WRITTEN IN LIEU OF AN ANTIWAR MARCH

Instead of marching today I will order a green tea and
some raisin walnut toast at the Parkside Cafe in Stinson
Beach, California, in my hand my blue plastic-wrapped copy
of the *New York Times* with a few raindrops clinging to it.

One of the locals in this little burg of 450 people will pass by my table,
smile, and tease, "There you are, reading your *New York Times*."

I should be mulching the garden or going to the fundraising
committee meeting for the new community center, or at the
very least taking care of the grandchildren.

But I open the *Times* and quietly as the fire leaps in one corner of my right
eye read on page A8 of the death of the Iraqi journalist Fakher Haider. I
think just last week he photographed the body of a fellow journalist, an
American freelancer, as it was unceremoniously stuffed into the back
of an army vehicle in a gray plastic sack and one could see the writer's
body...

I don't feel like marching today, I feel like weeping instead.
Why don't we have a big weep-in where we stand in a circle
with the dead man's beautiful 38-year-old face framed with
thick black hair and graced with a fluffy mustache above
the mouth that asked the wrong question, Daddy to three,
husband to one, the face that was bagged and shot, that
one, shot so we couldn't learn any more about Basra, and
the Iraqi police being infiltrated and by whom and how
the British are/are not handling it...

We could stand in a circle and just look at this man who by
all accounts went through his short life with quiet dignity
and a pen and a camera, words and images what he lived
and died for, we could just stand still for one moment
and weep for this.

PROVISIONS

"All that is solid melts into air, all that is holy is profaned, and man is at last compelled to face with sober senses his real conditions of life and his relations with his kind."
Marx and Engels, *The Communist Manifesto*,
as requoted in *The Earth Is Flat*, Thomas Friedman.

"Please do not flatten me into the pavement," I pray
to the god of those big rigs I name Goliath, all of them,
Goliath, Goliath as they speed toward me in nightmares or
pass so close I can feel their breath on Hiway 5...the goods
pouring into them over the internet and they googling each
other without drivers, reaching their holy consumers
eclipsing me in this game cooked up by New Delhi zippies
mirroring the mad trucks on the dirt road to the Taj Mahal
tinkling bells flying bright colors with frowns painted over
their cab windows shooting around the lurching camels and
donkeys while our driver's mother prays over her only son,
"Please do not flatten him into the road," she pleads with
Ganesh and pastes marigold petals onto the Elephant God's
bronze forehead with butter her worn brown hand gleaming
slipping down to her side, body wrapped in gold cloth for
her pilgrimage...
    "You are lucky," the California Highway Patrolwoman
consoles me "that I didn't have to scrape you off the
pavement," my heart pressed like a leaf under snow as I
watch the turquoise blue time capsule my Toyota the
last ten years of my life carried off so much scrap metal
the trucker from Walmart punching into his cell phone to
find out where the provisions need go next but unlike
David, the lowly shepherd, I have no biblical slingshot,
not even a stone to throw. . . "See Marx and Engels," Thomas

Friedman tosses off to me over his shoulder as he goes
online for his next airline ticket and in the Pakistani earth
cracks hideously open above where even Goliaths can
reach the terrified hamlets dissolving into dark laps of
the Himalayas. "Only a week before they freeze,"
we are told, the eye of the Buddha staring, staring over the last
ridge the hand of Allah caressing, caressing in small fires
the wounds of the screaming children. "Please do not
flatten us into the mountain," they pray mutely piecing
together rubble to blanket themselves inside of that last
crevasse where only photographers can fly to.

ON THE POET'S BIRTHDAY

for Jack

It's December again and my left
shoulder hurts the one I press the
world to as you always do seeing
more than what was meant thinking
deeper than what was thought
and as the full moon rises tonight
over the landward pounding sea I
know that your eye is constructing
a landscape of hope for the weary
and downtrodden and the poem lifts
its great arms to hug me, pressing me
into its chest as you did once lost child
that I was before I learned to take up
my pencil to love...

EATING FLOWERS
2004

EATING PIZZA WITH THE JEWS

for Daniel Pearl

The day I heard of your terrible end I was in Paris eating with my
six grandchildren in a kosher pizzeria not far from the Buttes
Chaumont...It was one of those gray sleety days. The rain blew up under
our hoods making our colds worse. I think we had a sore throat. I say
this in the collective because eating pizza with the Jews of Paris is a
collective experience. There's a virus in the gray buildings, under the
paving stones, in the ruins near the Marais that reaches so far back in
time. I've caught it even in the shadow of the Notre Dame Cathedral
at that park where the Holocaust Memorial reaches underground,
remembering for the French their deported countrymen (the word Jew is
not specifically mentioned).

The children ordered one tuna and olive pizza and three with just
cheese and tomato, the wind howled, our noses ran, your poor head
forced to say "I am a Jew, son of a Jewish Father" or whatever the exact
words were, now mixed in forever with the sniffles and the chills and
the image of another pizza parlor on King George Street, Jerusalem, that
went up not long ago body parts flying the odor of fire and flesh and
blood, once you've smelled this you are never the same. It imprints, and
flames are never the same again, nor is pizza ever quite the same. Today
I smelled it when I saw a knife, your brown curly-haired head slashed
off at the end of one story the long beginning of another as the children
bend their beautiful heads slightly to bless what we are about
to eat.

TO CAFÉ

for Na'ama HarEl and Roy Gordon

I want
to Café with you

that is the instant

when everything is calm

or as calm
as Café Moment
could ever be with
the traffic streaming
by and the cell phones being
jabbered into

"Cain" is the Hebrew
for "yes" and into
the cell phone the talker
goes "Ken, Ken, Ken,"

and "Lo" is the Hebrew
for "no" and into the
cell phone the answerer
goes "Lo,Lo,Lo!"

and in between

"Where are you?"
"What time will you

walk out of there?"
"What are you drinking
that made it worth
the journey there?"

"O'Fouk," it's the Hebrew
expression for "upside
down," and to drink white
latte on the bottom of brown
coffee so the latter floats onto
the former in a layer that barely
stays in place...

I once sat at Moment and ordered
mushrooms with a friend

we ate them and managed
to get through two love affairs
and a divorce, *"O'Fouk,"* it's
descriptive of a life, too, so
beautiful and nothing in the
right place.

Together we laugh we
laugh together

and the kid walks in with the bomb.

6/6/02

I WAS SWIMMING

I swam twenty laps
a measured even swim

with each breath I
took they were running
and dying diving and
dying, flying and dying
drifting through heaven
becoming angels of smoke
leaving their hands here
on earth, their legs, hair,
eyes, mounting on new
gray wings...

They changed worlds exploding
as I swam, my eyes open and trying to count
the little black tiles at the bottom in the long line
that separates me from the man swimming next to me
as they became my own unwitting sacrifice
going in place of me into the emptiness reserved
for objects of hate and their radiant tormentors

Their little desks climbed up freed of their papers
and their little chairs sailed into Nirvana

Someone bound her hands for me, the stewardess,
I mean, who had to suffer for me on a flight I did not
take because I lived heedlessly
on earth among the heedless

Oh they flew home from me as I swam twenty laps
and they became stars on the flag of the sky and the stripes
that scream blood and sorrow, blood and sorrow, those thirteen long
waving lines

I swam twenty laps and then floating for a moment
on my back I saw
how they loved one another in the black iron stairwells forever
and now
how they beckon to become love

in us all

BINYAMINA

for David Ehrlich

Just southeast of my favorite
beach in Israel lies a sleepy
town I once visited with you
and your little dog.

The three of us hiked
the surrounding hills,
pausing before a weathered
tower of yellow rock.

Such remnants are everywhere
in the holy land. Crusaders, Romans,
Turks, their hands piling the stone
one on top of the next, have created
these ruins under the shadow
of a warrior chief
standing over them.

"Build a place to shoot from," the shadow
would always order, in English, French, Latin,
or Turkish. "Build a place for us to see where
they are shooting us from."

The hillsides were pale green in Binyamina.
The little dog sniffed and peed on the side
 of the mighty rocks, built to survey or shoot the enemy.
We sat for a while in the silence and allowed the breeze of
Binyamina to whisper into our ears the eternal messages
of breezes: "Love one another. Respect one another.
Guard one another."

Today a suicide bomber and his Israeli soldiers left the train
station together, their souls swimming upward to the same
heaven. Binyamina.
That's all the sign said. It didn't say, Suicide Bombers,
to the left, Israeli Soldiers to the right. It simply said:
Binyamina.

July 16, 2001

TORTURE

I watch the small blue jellyfish
stranded along the tide line

babies big as my fingertip
and grown ovals the size
of a breakfast yolk before
being broken into by the tine
of a fork

the arc of tiny sails which
carried them over the waves when
they, too, were alive, bisecting their
bodies that pulse and glisten

into a thin blue wave dancing
as far as I can see
over the hard sand

All of them, children, adults
drying to thin, white wafers
moving slowly as the days pass
further inland

Perhaps today their deaths will reach
CNN or the newspapers and perhaps
by next month we will be given
the exact number. Someone will do
a story giving them a name, a date,
and the pain of their drying, a cause.

But now I can only face the sea, the
great wind, the ground too slippery
with them for me to even walk
all of this without a single sound...

In their silence I come to know
that there are more, countless more,
the blue turning shocking pink
and I have stumbled onto something
too terrible to even see or bear

TIGERS

"These are not jungle animals, they are royal beings."
Pankaj Joshi

I would have to disagree, given
what I now know about royalty
in India, the sumptuous
venal feasts in the harems

the bridal halls full of mirrors
and flickering flames concubines
being moved to and fro on a marble
Parcheesi board under the stars

and the garden where women danced
their clothes off under four lace
pavilions all at once

and the solitary stone dreaming chamber
with the bed raised so high, the ladder
removed each night so that whenever
King Akbar would raise his gun to shoot

the death that always stalks him
from behind would have to stop
and step out
of its shadow colored stripes
to eat.

MISSING MY LOVER

I am missing my
lover

How was I to know when he planted
that fruited kiss on my left
temple

and wrapped his good right arm
around me that in his left hand

he was reading his last instructions:

"Shine your shoes," they told him
"That you not go to Allah in shame..."

I weep for him in my bed of flowers
and my last smile hits the wall
shattering

into stones that clatter
against the ground,
tears of the diamond

Wife of God he gave up with one
eye fixed on the white scented
hems of women who came to him only
in dreams...

and who never made tea for him watching
his black lashes lower to the rim
of the cup, the steam oh rising like
a cloud a final cover for the face

of my beloved lover.

MAN OFFERING ME A BED OF GRASS

"Damn it, why aren't you
 in my bed with me?"

A sexy question,
a serious one.

I muse on it lying
on the grass under a black
pine tree, the noon sun smoking
through its needles of jade...

I can only answer with questions.

Do you carry a gun?
Can you control your anger?
Are you gentle?
Are you long-suffering/abundant
in all that is kind?

And I dreamt of an angry hare
last night! What alarmed
this small creature that
it would come all the way
from its world, its tender
green garden world where its pink
nose quivers at the touch of one blade
of grass into mine? What was it trying
to tell me? What was it longing
to say?

When we love ourselves
through the grass, its
creatures inform us.

And who are you kissing, love,
that's not God, not me.

MAN WALKING IN WATER, J.C.C., SAN RAFAEL, CALIFORNIA

Facing the doorway
leading out of the therapeutic
pool

a man is splashing at a terrific
pace in the water.

His dark brows are knit
his white hair curling
majestically above them...

Perhaps he is chewing on injustice
as he churns the blue square he's
been given to think in, not
water anymore, but unemployment, the
subject of his first book.

He's exposing the global capitalists as he
strides into his pages full
well knowing that others are walking the
same miles without this warm, forgiving
element surrounding their bodies,

grinding poverty instead, kept in place
by the forces he is treading against, trying
to name, as his feet pound the blue bottom, which in
his book is the opposite of imagination: the facts
he is seeking to gather this morning as he stomps
through the weightless wet.

THE GOD CAKE
2004

POEM IN WHICH I REMEMBER TRANSCENDENCE

Riding on the back
of a white eagle

or was I in the hold
of a silver jet parting
the clouds for an instant?

I looked down and spotted
the blue towel we lay on
in the green grass below

No, it wasn't an apple tree
a western wild lilac was shading
us

and in the rarefied silence
of the earthbound we could
feel moving over our sun-drenched
flesh the shadow of the wings we
would become as we flew away.

The bent grass mingled with wild
strawberries just that moment

exploding into red fruit

it unbent, the grass I mean,
and wept, as grass does,
for the heights we once reached
and the depths we once knew

down there.

ON THE FEAST OF MATZOS

On the feast of Matzos
I sat at a flowered table
and buttered the crisp

pages of poetry. I
ate them one by one
with the little holes
they make in them
to ensure that, no,
they will not rise

little holes in the matzos
little holes in the poems

eternity running through
them I ate the poems and
the matzos and then put
on a new suit and went to
say Kaddish for my father who
lies south of here, a whole
day's travel by car, in a desert
under black marble.

Perhaps the little stones I placed
on his grave last time are still
there, one from me, one from my mother,
to say to the silence that once was his
ear, "Plunk, plunk, Daddy, we're here."

Plunk, plunk.
Four deer came at me
this morning in the tall, windy grass,
their brown eyes falling into my soul
with the same sound
as the stones
on the grave of my father.

MORTALITY

Gray water in sheets over my windshield
on Highway 10l North
flooding as if the underworld
is surfacing to tell us one more time:

Love.
The heart pumps (this is abstract; I want
you to know it was coming out of my left arm
today in the bloodmobile, one pint from me
to you. They will begin marketing valentines
soon, won't they? But this is different.)

My hand reaching out of the open car door.

(Your tie looking like
a spider web on silk!

Your eyes above it, the argument
against reincarnation.

Saying we don't know that.
Saying look at me for ten seconds
and this has the power to transform
the rest of your life.)

The actors portraying A. E. Housman and
Oscar Wilde on stage at the Geary Theatre
today will both agree: "Love is a piece of
ice clutched in the hand of a child."

But that's not what I get.
My poem says love is the moment
before you pull it, your warm vital
hand, away from mine.

KABBALAH

Burdened by Eden
as I am

Empowered by twilight
enraged by wolves
as they dine
on small bellies

A nuthatch
signals me
from a blue bush

An owl sighs
and sinks
one wing
into the other world

Kingdom of dreams
and passages

Burdened with Eden
as I am
I touch the side
of your body
just under your
left arm

If one finger
of mine
just the side
of it brushed

the place I know well

You would rain forth
sweetness and be
redeemed.

WHAT TREES DO TO CARS

for Thomas Friedman

Trees shade cars.
The drivers pull them up
to their trunks on hot days
and they begin their movements

the shadows of leaves falling
everywhere on the dazzling paint
maple leaf on silver
oak leaf on hunter green
ginkgo on oyster white, and
on candy apple red, the combing
of Monterey pine needles...

The drivers lock, abandon
their vehicles and the leaves
sneak through to the interior

pressing their designs into
the upholstery the leaves
of an olive tree have even
been found, Thomas, under the
hood of a Lexus!

One leaf, well driven, has been
known to change the thought processes
of a car, moving its driver, awestruck,
helpless, into whole new worlds...

Trees do this all the time!

JEWEL AT THE BACK OF YOUR EYE

Creased as the emerald creases

Flashed as the fire-formed
flashes

Increased as wisdom increases
as pity and love increase
when fear has abated

Reflecting beauty as only
the illuminated can

Oh open your eye
a little more today won't you
where perhaps your grandfather
closed it, and let me in...

FOR THE WANT OF THIS GOOD SOUP

For the want of this good soup
a child is becoming stars today
a mother's head turning toward
the wall with a shade pulled down
between her and the world that spins
more slowly at her latitude more dizzyingly
more listlessly and fraught with the death
of so much soil

Small bodies are being washed today
with dust not water
with dust for the last time
for the want of this good bath

For the want of what is written
in this pot of soup, this tub full
of water, this dumb writing that my spoon
makes, that my body makes as it is flooded
with such fullness and weeps that it cannot
be shared.

BLOWING UP THE BUDDHA

for Bobby Wright

As you lay wasted
in those, your last days
on earth

The Taliban were busy, Bobby,
blowing up the Buddha as he
stood on the side of a mountain.

It was hard work, I gather, to
dynamite his huge legs, and the little
men must have looked like ants to him
in their attempts
to detonate all of that rock.

"No idols" say their sacred texts

So you entered eternity with him,
accompanied only by
the Buddha's smile.

March, 2001

TO MY RABBI THE ONE-MAN BAND

for Michael Barenbaum

I'm sitting at Noah's in Mill Valley. My laundry is in the machines down the street and I've just finished eating a whole-wheat sesame bagel with butter, toasted, for which I am grateful.

I have a short form of grace after meals. It goes like this: "God, please help me raise this food." I am writing this to you on three brown Noah's paper napkins.

I've just finished reading a newspaper article (*N.Y.Times*, p. 17, Section One) about the killings of five homeless men in the streets of Denver, Colorado.

The killings happened randomly. The men were found under loading docks, floating in the Platte River, and in an open field. None of them had money. What they had were names and ages:
Donald Dyer 51
George Worth 62
Melvin Washington 47
Milo Harris 52
Kenneth Rapp Jr. 43

The lone survivor of these attacks was sleeping when the assault on him began with one young man kicking him in the back before "five more come out of nowhere." He chased his assailants with a rock and survived.

Three of the dead men were his friends. He doesn't know if the young men in jail are the young men who killed them.

On Saturday morning at services you said you felt like a one-man band because of all of the things you were doing at once. Well, on the harmonica that's propped up and tied around your neck, could you please play a Kaddish for these, our middle-aged American homeless men who are killed "out of nowhere" because they have nowhere to go...?

THE PROPHETESS

for Shannon Wright

I have no problem, after centuries
of listening to their voices,
identifying your male counterparts.
But it's taken several hours, after
the newscasts, the tear gas, the arrests,
to identify you.

How did it feel to unfurl that banner
at the WTO conference yesterday in
Seattle after scaling that crane
in your climbing gear?

There is a light that surrounds those
moving toward God. It shines out of
a mind capable of making enough distinctions
then holding them taut, and acting out of
a body brave enough to match.

My friend with only one breast salutes
you. I'm having dinner with her tonight and
we will touch again on the insane statistics
in our neighborhood. One woman in every six.
It seems we can no longer filter our water
enough, while twenty-five-year-olds become
multi-millionaires overnight.

And I salute you. Every age needs its
prophetess. While climbing with two beautiful
breasts against the sky and a diploma from
Brown University between your eyes, did you
understand about being born into our world
with instructions?

I remember seeing you dressed, not in
biblical cloaks and rags, but in a smashing
cocktail dress at your sister's wedding.
You were turning to speak to someone, and
one bronze shoulder flashed, bare, the same
shoulder that pulled you up there yesterday
to say that money is not our God, and to
alert us below of the great wrongs which
you, from your millennial vantage point
with your eyes blazing the colors of our
earth and rain and trees, could see.

ON THE COLOR CORAL

It's cold and past midnight
I pull on a sweater of coral
wool and you slip into my dreaming
as if you have been waiting for the color
to call you from your other world, the world
you live and bathe and eat in.

Bathe? No. Shower. You always shower, I think,
and shake your hair dry like a sleek duck
coming up from a black pond...

Your arm is around me in the dream, darker than
life, Africa dark, and I am instructed not to be
afraid of this. As if I could be afraid
of your hand dripping down like it does
over the back of my coral sweater, the last two
fingers joined together by a golden ring
shaped like a small picture frame.

Above us is a hill where our two spirit trees stand
at the top in dream-shadow black, with a miniature
of my house, painted yellow and coral as it is now,
sitting under them.

But now that I think of it again, it was not a
picture frame at all, that golden ring on your last
two fingers. It was a copy of this page which holds
the wealth of all we have refused to desecrate
by the form we have chosen for our love.

FAWN CROSSING INTO IVY

Yesterday I turned onto the street
that runs behind our high school

The parking lot was crammed with
the cars of our young at study

The ordinariness of the day,
the ordinariness of the parked cars.

I slowed to permit a young deer
to cross the street in front of
my car. There's a moment when
a deer looks me in the eye

admitting me into deer world.
We live with them moving in
and out of the boundaries
of our gardens

They eat our prize roses and bear
their fawns onto beds of fern
under our trees

I remember a mother deer in my garden
nursing twins the day my son graduated
from this high school. She had eaten
every apple off my small tree and
was converting it to deer milk.

My son gave the speech at his graduation.
He stood there without bullet holes
in his beautiful young body. He had made
the best of his life after the divorce,
picking his way gently among the fallen
branches

This young deer
steps delicately off
of the asphalt into
the ivy at the side
of the street, moving
with an eyeblink into

eternity

where our nation has buried
the sons and daughters and
teachers who on such an ordinary
day, with their cars all parked

neatly in rows, were sent
by the deranged among us.

It's green and silent
in the Garden of Eden.
The pages of the textbooks,
open, absorb rain in the
curious half-light. Perhaps
the dead children are studying
with their dead teacher, who
tried to protect them. Studying
the huge cracks in our life,
and the ways we try to ignore
them.

There's a gust of wind.
The leaves from their world
blow into ours in a jeweled
shower of red (their maples)
and yellow (their poplars.)
They land on the pavement
accompanied by silent prayers
(Yes, the dead pray to us) that
we screech to a halt and try
to read them and absorb
their transparent, urgent lessons.

Mill Valley
December, 1999

BIRD WITH BLUE (MY) EYES/POEMS OF SAFED
2002

WHILE THE MEN PRAYED

While the men prayed
I chose to walk
past the graves
of this city

past the brave
who are counted
and the murdered
children

A small blue door
was ajar
within the courtyard
a woman sat in a red dress
and stared at her plate

the large sabra cactus at
her gate had yellow blossoms

which grew red and exploded
before my very eyes

While the men prayed
I chose to walk
to let my feet
witness what their God

held under his right arm
as he gathered their prayers
under his left

IN THE OLD MOSQUE

In the old mosque
the artists of Safed
have their collective
exhibition

All I could think
of was my lover

As I roamed through
everyone's passionate

gaze trapped and painted
then hung in the place

where the Arabs of Safed
once prayed to their God

a poem ran from my lips
to my absent one
like a sparrow trapped
in the old mosque and
flew in and out among
the paintings and ghost-
white prayers.

When I could no longer
breathe I made for the
sunlight, released the
poem into the sky.

Just like a sparrow
that finds another on
a high wire my poem
brushed the little feathered
body of my lover with its
soft beak of delight.

A HARD DAY FOR THE ARI

At his big blue painted tomb
with prayer books spread over
it, the Ari was having a hard
day.

Master of cabalistic lore
and rabbinic commentary he
first had to pose for pictures
with a busload from eastern
Europe. He had to hear his
story told, over and over,
in seven different tongues,
of how the dream came to him
in Egypt and told him to come
to Safed.

The tale of his brilliance was
embellished until his ears rang
from eternity. The sorrow of his
passing at only thirty-eight was
mourned until he thought, "Enough!"

Then as they prayed, people wept. Wax
dripped down from all of the candles.
He bestirred his wonderful mantle
of love and it shone forth out of
the grave for those who could
touch such things with their eyes.

He healed with a blue laugh that was
a joy to hear. All of this took energy.
As the sun sank under Mt. Meron, he stretched
forth his fingers of pink light to enter
the evening prayers in all of the synagogues
that bore his name
(He was a great egalitarian)
and even counseled the women in their
kitchens not to get angry, The Shechina was,
after all, among them. He tended children lost
and crying in their beds from the strain
of so much learning. And, at last, in the
darkness, when the final candle had wept
itself out, he

shimmered down into the easy sleep
of the just and truly happy.

THE SWEETNESS PROBLEM

The men are told
they should not
covet the sweetness
of another man's
wife.

It is left
for future commentary
to teach them
to sweeten their own
wives until they sing
like angels in their beds.

Once the wife problem
is solved, we contemplate
the widow and divorcée problem,
the gorgeous young virgin
problem, not to mention other
men.

The sweetness problem would
not go away, so next to the
law and the commentary,
God invented poetry.

AN ABSTRACT PAINTING

Just under the surface
of that squashed piece
of magenta

I detected an old army
uniform lying on its side

the insignia couldn't
be deciphered; a blur
of red outlined in gold,
it could have been anything.

I didn't know what to love
or fear, and, besides, the
uniform blocked the inner light
of the canvas.

so I left the painting alone.

ON LEAVING A FRIEND

for Michal Auerbach

Dividing the sky into squares
the bare arbor stands above
us on your rooftop

each space a poem of mine not
to be written there

or a canvas
you are yet to fill.

As the swallows carve patterns
across the blue-green metal frames,
their tails circle the moon, little
forks of the dispossessed who gesture
toward a fading silver plate they
know they will never eat from...

The same grapevine that dips
into the bathroom window
is reaching its tendrils

upward toward the arbor where
we sit eating from a bowl of
fresh carrot salad in the evening
wind.

Fractures of light
are filling the windows
of Safed above us, cut

glass washed with colors
found only in the eyes of
dreamers or weepers or those
who glory in something we
can only begin to see.

SHARDS

The old walls are topped
with broken glass

I am looking down on
one this morning
So this is what protects me
now. Blue, green, what they
used to carry, wine, olive
oil, water, long gone. Were
they deliberately smashed?

They stand like pieces of
an old womb whose children
cannot love it.

ANTIGONE AND APHRODITE/POEMS OF CORFU
2001

A CLOUD, 1/2 MOON

A cloud, 1/2 moon,
a pile of sand being
raised to a high window
in a black leather bucket

a street-side shelf
of small pies,
a broken door with
a broken handle, a perfectly
painted vanilla-colored mansion
in the style of the Venetians,
leather, lace, gold-sellers, silver-
sellers, a case full of aromatic
candles, Homer, Virgil, George
Seferis, Yannis Ritsos, the sea with
the sun and rain plunking into it

but, no you.

IF WE RETURN

I will say this
on a clear day
when the Island stretches
its multiple glories outward

when there are patches
of milk white on the waters
over cinnamon blue

I will say this
in the presence of such
wild iris poking out
of even the gravel, three,
four on one stem

and a sky marred by
only two clouds just now
streaking
like frilly bombs
toward Albania...

If we return
out of love for this Island
and to remember it

You will know us

We will be the ones
some of you despised.

FULL MOON, PYRGI

Someone thin, silent as a cat
was sitting on a low pink wall
as I passed by

His hair was wild and long
and black, his beard had
a huge gash of moonlight

through it, and his dark
sad eyes moved quietly
to my face.

THE GOD OF WAR
2001

The face you saw
with its two teeth
of ivory
growing down
into my lower
lip

and spoke to
with the thunder
of purchase

was not my face.

My face cannot
be bought.

At Sinai
with a monastery
cut into its belly

from this mountain

with smoke and cloud
and a male voice that
incises stone

with thunder and
rain clinging to
his horns of light

Moses descended

to talk to the men
a little about
how to treat their
women

I wept for the dead
of the God of War
as he lay across
my body a bomb
in one hand a cigarette
in the other

arched in his spasm
of terror delight
and oblivion

I rained kisses
onto his breastbone
and whispered
to his heart

that if he dropped
the cigarette onto
the carpet
we would not burn up.

This was necessary
before I could
disarm him.

All of the stoplights
in the nation have turned
from red to bright orange

The president stands
a New Age general making
war in a suit and tie

the lights of the red glossy
cover of *Time* magazine focus

on the face of a young woman
they have captured at his
side

a baby whale dies on a
small coastal island, of
poisons too deep to name or
winds too strong to withstand.

A tree, black oak, redwood,
magnolia, or pine, I am confused,
what tree, where? is falling...

Beneath the level of language
where words are waves that
telegraph motion and light

against that thick brown back-
ground your arm is stretched
out toward your proud black
horse

you are wearing a white shirt

this painting is centuries old
and yet your shirt glows

the gesture
of the outstretched arm
is the gesture
of the outstretched arm
is the gesture
of the outstretched
arm.

THE DIG AT EIN GEDI
2001

THE SIBYL AT EIN GEDI

Each morning here we fit our hands into a different pair of gardening gloves, and on occasion, I've come up with a thumb missing, or a seam split. There's a hectic grabbing of tools. No one wants the pickaxe that loses its head in the dust or the most bedraggled of brooms, or the buckets that can't hold their handles upright.

So the first thing I noticed about her was that her gloves were intact.

She popped up from the site next to mine, pulled off a glove, and with the one bare hand over her eyes to shade them, stared for a long moment at the Dead Sea, and Jordan, emerging from piles of blue-grey clouds, on the other side.

The dust burrows into our clothes here, glazing them to colors we most often see in dreams.

Last night I dreamt I was floating in layers; we were all on our backs according to generation: my daughter and her daughter lay above me, my mother and her mother, beneath. We breathed gently and floated in the sea. Then a brown head came barreling toward us; he was swimming furiously, looked like my brother, splashing like at an Olympic swim meet. His head tore into us, and we were hurled into a spin, somersaulting over and over in the sea. We couldn't surface or breathe, or even separate back out, but spun there, all our ages mixing and churning under the water.

The Sibyl stared at us, a wordless witness.

Her feet planted firmly in the Byzantine, her brown-cropped hair blowing in a morning breeze that just might herald the millennium. Her two breasts under the cerulean cotton shirt, her shaded eyes, and a blood-red sweater wrapped around her waist at grave level.

From that point, as far as my own eye could see, was the tumbling brown earth we have come to confuse here with History

And with time.

ANIMAL FRAGMENT

Lunching with the Essenes
sitting on warm stones
with packets of egg and cheese

Blue Jordan spread out in the
distance waiting for its dying
King to fly home

The palm grove below
the size of a large hand
and our dig
at the village of Ein Gedi,
the clipboards, buckets
and humans, looking like an
insect pursuit

We contemplate the fragment
of an ibex horn roughly torn
or hacked from its head,
found on the floor of a cave.

I am not speaking of History
here; Josephus is silent on the
subject of dreams, nor does he
describe one birth among all the
butchery

We know nothing
of how they ate
their lives and staring
over what they stared
over I can only say
that someone once sat here,
freshly dipped in this pool
of spring water, eating an egg,
perhaps, and, pondering his origins,
imagined a large hand planting
the trees below. And, for lack of a
better word, referred to that someone
as "He."

OH.

Smaller than the entrance
to the wasp's nest, the pupil
of my eye has learned to contract
and see into the minuscule

I sit for hours in one corner
of one room sifting dust
for vital information.

Whether the goblet is half
empty or half full is not
the issue, both joy and sorrow
being too large to contemplate
here...

I am holding the open mouthbone
of a strange little fish in my
palm, the tiny rounded teeth still
attached to it. After the wars,
pillage, the smoke-soaked layers
surveying their frequency, this
tenacious fragment of a whole mouth
that ate and was eaten by another
mouth.

The song of a mouth into nothing,
it rests on my palm as a challenge.
Name one thing that lasts beyond
dust. When your jaw no longer
moves, and both going in and coming
out are banished. What then, poet,
will you say?

Ein Gedi.
Ein Gedi.
Ein Gedi.
Spring of the young kid
That's me.

TAMBOURINE
2000

WINGS OF ANOTHER ERA

I. Flight

Into the waning months
toward the millennium
Into the flat corridors
of silent cloud
the jet stream
heavy with cargo

Our giant wings
flop and rattle
We bend over
small dinners
red wine rolling
down the aisles
and white; champagne
in small bottles

while two faces bend
toward each other

is it Hugh Grant?
is it Julia Roberts?

a child's hand is sliced
by barbed wire at the UN
compound in East Timor

another face, that of a baby,
surfaces from the rubble
of the earthquake in Taiwan

the horrid wars mix with the grinding
of the earth's plates as, flame-like,
a wing from another era moves
into the night side of the earth

crumpled, wet, as if newborn,
crumbling around the edges
as if ancient stone-carved
and veined

with the pale tragedies
that sing into the dark
wind always at our backs

lips from another era press
into mine from behind my face

to write from the lips of others
is considered a sacred act
in any age

Silently, steadily, yellow candles
burn down and we guide our planeloads
toward the airport.

If they would stop trying
to sleep through the flight
they would feel us everywhere
rising over tears and honor, screams
and the stopping of a single breath
coloring the tips of our feathers

gold.

II. BODIES

There are hollows
in my body
that will never
be filled

Places where you have
grazed with small pearls for
teeth as they once surfaced in
my hand at the dig at Ein Gedi

Small pearl teeth
set into a palate
of dusty ivory

I have seen you moving over me
soft black fur sprouting like
delicate moss touching your flesh
curling around it. Each hair on your
body lifting it into a breeze that
surrounded you.

To be touched again by that breeze
I would need to fly back
toward you, the centuries
falling away.

Ah, your knee, only that
rising in marble

Ah, your throat,
only that, in granite

Only your belly in onyx,
only your shoulder, the right
one, in chalk.

Were all of this to crumble,
the dust of it would not fill
the spaces
where you have touched me
and fled.

Fleeing becomes you.

Then your black hair streams back
from your brow and your lax
palm confronts the next century,
fingertips not reaching out
but curling elegantly
beckoning no one.

III. POEM FOR AN AUGUST BRIDE

for Sana James

On a clear dark night
in years to come
perhaps I will look
out onto the San Francisco Bay

A boat will come
into being, a Ferry
as in all important moments,
there's a Ferry!

The Greeks knew of this,
cloaked their endings in dark
waves with a light
known only to them.

A beginning is when
the boat turns suddenly, the
light the same, the waves the
same, but jewelry spills out
from every shore into time.

We mark such beginnings
with laughter.

IV. FOR ANNE, CYCLING IN VIRGINIA

in memory of Anne Neeley

I always imagined
that green leaves
were a little greener
for you

and somehow all of that
speed and light went into
your personal window
of exhilaration to create

a super technicolor world!

Your words were like that;
warm and spiced with intense
feeling...

When we cannot ask more time,
depth is the bottom line, Anne.
I remember you diving off a
high bridge into a small deep pool
at the Trinity River one summer

Goddesses of the ancient world were
born that way, coming up out of the
green water with their lips parted,
tossing diamonds out of their short
sculpted hair

Born to challenge us, the flame buried
behind their faces, a flame whose meaning
we are left to discover as we stare
at their gorgeous enigmatic presences
surfacing broken from the rubble of ages

Dust to dust, yes, but out of dust
these holy faces of the feminine are pushed
forward to reveal us to ourselves . . .

When you woke into your greenest morning
pushed your silver wheels toward it
and were slammed into the planet in a new way

I like to think
that you rose to the challenge as always, and,
instead of stopping, you sped into the elements
so that now as I sit before this green tree,
this blue sky, this small toast-colored road,
I think Anne, Anne, Anne.

V. THE FACE AT ZIPPORI

for Tina Chase

1.

The emblem of this ancient city
a beautiful Roman woman
fixes us with her brown gaze,
one eyebrow lifted slightly over
a few mosaics flown off into the
ages exposing the hard-packed
Galilee cement onto which she was
composed.

Designed in earthtones as you are,
her brown hair is elegantly coifed,
and, falling from each ear, an earring
of coral, white, and gold.

She addresses me full face as you do
a small replica of Eros standing
on her right shoulder his bow pulled taut.

How often we have spoken of him in
some guise or another, husband, lover,
son.

And out of the surrounding hunt, of
birds and beasts embedded in the black
chips of an ancient sky, she tells me,
as you often do, that these moments can
be shot with light instead of arrows,
and that the hunt can become a sacred
dance.

The artisans of Zippori set a wreath of
laurel leaves into her braids and twists
of hair. Each leaf can be brushed with
water to shine again, that
we read them, and slowly come to see
what she lived, what we live.

2.

If she lived, she came, perhaps, in a time
of conquest to this high plateau overlooking
four valleys. Did her husband wash his blood-
stained hands in this cold spring water? The
graves surround Zippori in the farthest
perimeters. Was she familiar with them?
Did she go there in the end, or back to Rome?

I like to imagine that we were friends then,
too, a friendship leaping all barriers as I
walked one day up from the neighboring Jewish
quarter. Perhaps we met in a flash of recognition
in the narrow streets of Zippori as we once did
in a public park. If someone had told me then,
"you are about to meet an eternal friend," would
I have stopped pushing my child on the swing for
an instant and recorded your face, the leaves
of the bay laurel tree pressing against your
20th century brow with flickerings of light?

3.

As I stand on scaffolding around the living room
floor in which she is embedded, I imagine you and I
here. I've just come in parched from the heat and
we are sitting on pillows and drinking chilled wine.

The mosaic on your living room floor teaches
us of the god Dionysos, and shows the horrors
of drunkenness. Herakles is sloppy drunk on
your stone carpet!

Did we slyly laugh at this? Or were we too repressed?
The winds of this place are hot and dry in June. A bird
sounds as it must have sounded while we tried to share
our hearts in the hot silence. Were there servants
listening? Was I, a Jew, even allowed into the mansion?

Or perhaps I came here merely to deliver something to
you. A piece of woven work, or a bit of pottery or glass.

Was there again, as these objects passed from my
hand to yours, that flicker of eternal recognition?
My friend, my star, my time...

June l999
Jerusalem

POEMS OF MY SPANISH SUMMER
1998

A man is singing
in what once was
a synagogue, his
voice crying into
the rafters of cedar
and mother-of-pearl

the words stop
and fall to the ground
small white tears
carved from the flesh
of the ancient trees
that once came by sea

to this place of stone
and silence

renamed now for the death
of a countrywoman said
to have given birth
to a dying god.

I fly through the cathedral
on tiny bat wings
(we can change shape,
you know!)

Here are pieces
of light that dazzle
cut glass from the
penitents of Toledo

I spread them out
into the small streets
beneath it.

For every sigh
of torment that
was uttered here

in the name of a
suffering God who
once was a Jew

I am removing a piece
of light
from this grand
cathedral.

And for each tortured man,
woman or child this place
loses more pieces of light

soaked into my wings
for eternity.

EL TORO BLANCO

I was calved
in the southern
swamplands

among the hard
warm bodies
of my cousins

I grew on sunlight
and shadow, and
the mists as they
entered my nostrils

I know nothing of
flag or country

and am innocent
of butchery.

I float over my
dying body, its cape
of blood which pours
down my sides

and rise out of the
bullring of Córdoba
like a cloud begging
for rain

The crowd chants to its
proud matador, and the
bands sing as if at
fiesta:

I rise up out of the bullring
of Córdoba, but the sky
is no place for a bull.

My sides are wrapped
onto a tower
My cape of blood follows
me there
You can see me through
all of your *calles*
where I am standing again
at the end...

I am not an apparition
of kindness
and my wrath has
kindled disdain

A stone horse will pour
me some water
a jeweled virgin
will feed me some grain.

Somewhere in one of your
castles
a woman starves on bread behind
bars
Somewhere in one of your
gardens
Two shadows are plotting
deceit

My tower of gold
will sink slowly
down into the river
below

As all of your greatness
will crumble
before my bones have seeped
into sand.

PAINTING IN THE DARK
1998

I am supposed
to kiss you goodbye

but as I sit
within a dark jet

on a darker air
field (we have landed
on a Greek Island, love,
so the airlanes will be
clear tonight for the
bombing of Iraq)

waiting in the dark
on a dark air field
on this dark island
I decide

time and space have stolen
enough from me, you I am keeping
forever.

Your open mouth
was trying to say
one last thing

it tried and tried
until it became this
small fir tree

which each year
will grow a little
taller in the absence
that was you.

Tonight it freezes
unaccustomed
to the sudden drop
in temperature

but already it is
sending slender
messages
from my world
into yours.

I dreamt your face
with little black
holes

In them
were all the truths
you withheld from me.

I stared into this face
which frowned
around a headache

fires burned our two flags
on TV and missiles were
sharpened like pencils signing
death warrants.

I finally decided
that the holes
were places you could not
afford, for one reason
or another, to remove
your black mask from.

Beneath each word
I write to you
a pair of black and white
wings
hang
as if dead:

phantom of desire
form minus the content

while you stand
in a black and white
tuxedo before a large
bunch of white lilies
oh gorgeous butterfly...

On my return to Jerusalem
I kissed the corner of the
Jaffa Gate
smeared with red and blue
paint and scored
with bullet holes

It's well known that
red on city walls and
flags displays:
what our hearts pump
can also destroy us.

Lesser known: that blue
keeps away mosquitoes
and the small stabs
of indifference which
also divide and kill.

MEMORIAL SERVICE/POEMS OF ARAD
1997

A CAMEL IS KNEELING ON THE FAR END OF THE WORLD

The smallest house
I've yet to live in

And my bed slopes
downhill

Just to the left
of my head
in the dark
a camel
is kneeling

The white one
I saw grazing.
The one whose head
disappeared onto the
other side of the world.

And when I looked
toward the kitchenette
one half of the moon turned
the corner from the bathroom
window between the needles
of a pine branch
and managed to pour
one teaspoonful of
light onto the camel.

OASIS AND DESIRE

I want to start with the sun
on the honey-colored rock
(because it was so hard to
create a silence in this place

with the tourists in bathing suits
and the busloads of school children,
the staff with cellular phones)

and although an oasis is the water
tumbling through the rock cleft
behind itself, a double waterfall

the rock moves up through light
bright and awesome caves dent
its face with their black
mouths

We sat still, and that is
the point of the journey
until we saw the babies eating
Sodom apples and their mothers
shaking them free from full
udders as they tried to mount
the high places...and that
show stopper of all time as he
leapt from crag to crag causing
honeyfalls of stone his rough
banded horns arching over his
head and his beard like King
Tut's only tinier and thinner

Primacy: I am golden, I am swift,
I want that female, that high
place, that end

THE SHEEP, THE CAMELS

The sheep have suddenly
turned into money

A tall Bedouin stands
before the bank in the
sun and slowly counts
his cash

His crisp white mustache
His long, tan skirt
His white head scarf
His black shoes
His brown one-hundred-
shekel bills in a three-
inch-thick stack.
The sheep, the camels
are gone from the bald
hills to the place of
shearing and slaughter
that I may sit on a carpet
of camel hair that took
two women five years of
their lives to weave.

A CHILD, A GRAVE, A BORDER

She was the epitome
of innocence as she
stood, in a small
dress as befits a child,
her face slightly upturned

She was running toward
the border which was marked
with a gray gravestone

a butterfly had already
crossed over to our side

"Gaza" was what it said
on the gravestone, and
that is the last piece
of information I can give

Her mother yelled "Stop!"
and ran to drag her back
from the freedoms we imagine
ourselves to have.

The rest of the poem is questions.
       Why a girl child?
       Why a gravestone?
       Why "Gaza"?

WE PLANT CHILDREN

In this nation
we plant children
I cannot walk
past a new pine tree
without pressing into
its roots with my lips
of song

They grow young
and fine

Then, arms around each
other, they go to war.

Each year we visit the
cemetery here on Memorial
Day and the children in the
eleventh grade have the honor
of standing silently in
memory of the fallen: their
classmates, who sleep under
the blazing white stone
blankets. With their courage
we have purchased more children.
And houses for them. Gardens.
And walkways of stone.

The children swim in the bright
blue pool today. The water slides
over their backs and under their
hearts.

The wind ripples the water.
The trees and roses blow
in the bright, dry air.

Each standing child represents
a fallen child. Thus our numbers
have a different meaning here.

ON THE HIGHWAY

Passing the sand
dunes near Ashkelon

I try not to crash
as I watch the two
war planes training
soldiers to jump into
the sky, pull their cords
and float down...

Quicker than I can
count them the brown
jellyfish pull out
from under the silver
belly

each of them
dangles
a real live boy
with blood pressure
and a birthdate, and,
somewhere, a real live
mother, trying not to
crash as she lives this.

JUST LIKE IN THE SONG OF SONGS
2009

I GOOGLED HOLINESS

"I googled 'holiness,'" confessed the bar mitzvah
boy laughing in his new suit standing with his
parents on the bimah about to read the portion we Jews call
Kedoshim, the holiness code, and wanting to say something
about his subject before he plunged into the text unrolled
before him, the parchment dancing with Hebrew letters inked
by the hand of the *sofer* who bathed to purify himself in preparation,
said the proscribed prayers, and with utmost
concentration, faced the very space the young man was about to enter.
If one mistake had been made in the Torah transcription, the entire text
would have to be rendered unfit and buried as if it had been a person.

Thus not understanding that he was about to perform open heart surgery
on his great-grandmother, the bar mitzvah boy could laugh.

ON THE DUMPING OF MILK

With a cupful of milk and anything on your shelf like a few
strands of spaghetti and a leftover tomato you can make a
soup, a good one that warms the being and makes it feel all
rosy and content, which is what all beings deserve whatever
the dice has thrown them, a rundown overcrowded
apartment, a cardboard box under a freeway overpass, a
thorn bush in the dust with a bright cloth pulled over it, so
there oughta be a law put onto the international books that a
prosperous country like modern Germany for example not
allow striking dairymen to dump their milk, some protocol
put in place, an aqueduct built, or a dam, preferably near a
port city so the good ship milk could sail out on that sea of
hunger the world's children are lying on the beach suffering
wave after wave

of

With a cupful of milk and a can of creamed corn, you could make a soup, a
good one, one that warms the being and makes it feel all sunny and content,
which is what all beings deserve...

With a cupful of milk and a spoonful of wheat, corn, or rice you could make a
porridge, a good one, one that warms the small being with the morning sun

of hope.

TO AN OUD WHILE SITTING IN MONTCLAIR, CALIFORNIA

In this throat at the open neck of this street which comes to a V
at a Starbucks coffee shop in a free city in a free state of a free nation,
something is missing, the canned refrain blares out of the small speakers,
cars roll past this sound, what *is* it, without the beautiful carved instrument
strung in dim stone corridors behind bazaars bombed out, raided, where
religious police roam to stamp out more black notes, sparks of fires that
burn in the soul and will not die…

At the border they snatched up his oud, the one made by the
the master Mohammed Fadhel. So lovely and deep he slept with it
and his parents worried about this. *I went on to Jordan*, he reported,
but this was the saddest moment of my life.

And I remember sitting in Paul's Café, the Marais, Rani's eyes filling
with tears as he heard his old uncle playing the oud and singing
the songs his Algerian grandmother used to sing to him while here
at Starbucks, at the throat of the street neck of cement, an oud wails
out of the loudspeaker like the mouth of a ghost separated from its
mother, weeping out, trying to find her.

FOR HANNAH CROSSING INTO SNOW

We who are left
trace your footsteps
into the snow bank
seeking the diamonds
scattered across your back

stars entering your eyes
the liquid ice of love spilling
across darkening space

car and driver
who spun into you in wicked
Manhattan street narrative melting into
shadow having no place in this memorial
we are constructing of honor and goodness
and bright.

We count your brief seasons relishing
your deep smiles, your strength, wisdom
startling in one so young, your beauty breaking
into pieces for us to light and place
sparkling standing now in this bank of
January snow.

TANGO-ING AWAY FROM YOU

"In tango, one is always halting, dragging something, look,
now my toe is dead and I'm dragging it."
Glenn Corteza

I practice this dragging step high over
the Trinity River on a wide footbridge
to my cabin the water disturbed and tumbling
over the bed of rock sounding in my ears

With each step I am tango-ing away from you,
step, drag, halt, the dead toe being pulled
slowly onto the imaginary line I'm making
crossing
the river, all that we were moving
swiftly downstream toward the shrinking lake,
drained to make fountains, full swimming pools
green lawns in Southern California.

There you go, love, silver, laughing merrily on your way to
my past, the LA River winding in a concrete culvert not far
from where I once taught high school. Step, drag, halt,
now the big toe is in junior high school with you, let's
stop, leave you there, that's just how you left me, like a kid
from junior high school full of fresh kisses for his next love.

CARVED IN STONE

For "Baraso," Abdul Razzaq Hekmati

(1)

Judgment time. I need to decide whether or not you were cruel
silver mask over your face, your lips solemn under it
brown eyes glistening out of it like — eyes.

You flew up in a graceful movement past the huge window so I could have
a good long look, black cape curling in the wind like the tail of a huge ray
fish would have done, had it been water...

(2)

"You *should* be afraid of me," you said languidly.
 "That's just a masque," I countered, waiting for your
silver face to crack.

(3)

120 miles per hour is not too fast for you, but it is for me.
What is it with the speed trip, the black desert whipping its
winds past White Sands, test strip for the death wish, the end
of all worlds?

(4)

"Remember Paris," you said when you ended "it,"
meaning me, and I thought, Paris? But it was New Mexico!
Three Rivers, the petroglyphs, remember?

(5)

Maybe that's why they carved them in stone, the sacrificial bighorn sheep
with three arrows in it, the sun in the circle, the reverse wave, the hand
raising its six-fingered hello/goodbye, and the thunderbird, caught there,
moving on stone upward like you did in my dream, the stone-age artists
so in love with life and the universe and shocked at what those living
among them, beyond them, might actually forget.

(6)

"Let your heart break," read the poet after the rainstorm last night to
rainbow a covenant between me and my suffering, scooping words off the
lively paper under dim lights at the Café Trieste, "that you may feel even
more for others."

So I let you fly off to Belize, Thunderbird, with your arm around her,
and turn my tear-spattered windshield toward that barbed wire cruelty,
Guantanamo Bay where lies Baraso, "Arm" as his countrymen nicknamed
this war hero in their Afghani streets for his daring deeds, jail busts for two
counter-Taliban highly placed government officials who would testify for
him in a New York minute. Too bad the powers detaining him couldn't
even wait that long to weave his shroud out of lies. Speaking of this, what
do you tell her about me, and why are you letting me vanish in a shack in
the glaring sun surrounded by a strange sea so many miles from home?
I sorrow for him, accused, undefended, persecuted, and most probably
tortured, all we don't want to think of, you two with your suitcases
opening the door to that room where I'll die, *his* remains, will they even
be mentioned?

Baraso, why didn't your friends, the ones you risked your life for, come
for you, take to those same streets where they named you, shout out over
international TV, Baraso, Baraso, We Want You Free! And who did *I*
vote for? I saw no one on my ballot who even mentions your name, much
less someone who could get down on his/her knees and crawl to your
family, beg their forgiveness for the cancer that's eating up justice in
Guantanamo Bay, Baraso, making its quick meal, though we don't like to
think of this, of you, love, of you, Baraso, with your brave and brotherly
arm, sacrificial bighorn sheep with three arrows in it, of you.

6 February, '08

THE ABSOLUTELY LAST POEM
I'LL EVER WRITE ABOUT YOU

This poem begins in a dawn-colored room
(the windows rimmed in bright green paint)
in the high desert.

We were reading in bed, and I interrupted you to say something,
       so
you put your finger on a word in the upper middle of the page
and looked over at me, still fully absorbed by what you were reading,
your mouth a little "o," your lovely eyes close upon me.

I don't remember my question. We drove all the way back to where
my own car was parked that day. But before we did, we settled up. I gave
you a personal check for half the rooms, half the foods, and half the
gases. As soon as I handed it to you, you kissed me, a long, expressive,
talking, moving kiss, very unlike all the others. "Wow!" I thought. This is
not about love, it's about the rooms, the foods, the gases, and I want to ask
you, say, what was the word, not love, that you put your finger on that
morning in the middle of the page in the high desert dawn-colored room,
the windows full of bright green paint at the end of this poem?

LAST TANGO IN BUENOS AIRES

What if you met him only once

But this is so Romantic what if
you met him only once you were sitting
 in a blouse of gold leaves
at the edge of a ballroom
sitting watching
the tango dancers at the old *Confiteria Ideal*
with its marble columns its polished wooden floor its baroque ceiling
arabesquing above you and the little puffs of air
coming from the hidden fans swirling the skirts of the bare-
shouldered women up up to the edge of their panties and down but this is
so old Hollywood so film-like the dim
ancient lighting fixtures casting their receding glow...

What if you met him only once as you sipped your 7UP
in a crinkled glass and out of some dark corner he pounced
into the only other chair suitably ornate, the chair, not him,
black patent leather shoes tight black pants all six feet
of him dressed in an open-necked shirt with a little dot
of turquoise on a chain at his throat something of a gray
moustached jaguar about him and the two of you to the strains of violins
and piano the bandoneon of Astor Piazzolla began that long conversation
that has yet to end "But I thought you had *forgotten* me, Lady," said
yesterday's email, what if only once and you spoke of all that is really
important in a life at that tiny table, of loves gone by and the most ancient
practice of killing the young and brave in the planet's endless wars...

What if he asked "And you, have you found no one else to love my lady?"
just before he lifted you up in his long arms and spun you out onto the
glittering floor...

SOME WORDS ON DESTINY

> "That's what Destiny means: being opposite,
> and nothing else, and always opposite."
> *The Duino Elegies*, Rilke

They were your words, love,
"I think Destiny introduced us
in one unthinking moment."

For Destiny it's easier, like the wink
of an eye, to stop its thought, all
thought, and let the pure space
pour through its windy blue cage
of meaning.

And I thought to unthink myself
for only then could I truly meet you
once again.

Could I hold in the palm of my hand
such newborn tenderness, eyeless,
with its pale pink ears erect to take
in the music, the sound of a kiss
we've yet to take? All we've done is
dance a little dance, talk a little talk,
and part...

Destiny blinked, and in that one blind
unknowing, put your eye to my eye, love,
and directed us to begin the long drinking
of each other, within...

UNDER YOUR WHITE HAIR

Under your white hair
your brow, in the center of your brow
your third eye, pure consciousness,
the place from which you say to me "I love you,"
the same place where the blue sky has always been since you took
your young pen up close to the killing your white hair now
springing up so lovely and lively
like a cloud moving over the site of a rape in Darfur today and its
attendant butchery

no more not then not now not ever
I love you end the killing now…

FOR YOU IN THE DARK WITH A COKE

Such a tiny frame of the film of you, grainy because I cannot see all the way to Avenida Mitre, Buenos Aires, the place where you are walking cell phone in one hand, Coca-Cola in the other. While we speak you take a sip and I hear it, such a small thing, but it's the first time I've ever heard you drink, the Coca-Cola sliding down your throat to become Marcelo walking, and I can imagine your feet on the pavement, the same ones that were planted before me dressed in black patent leather grazing the bottom of the seashell-tinted ballroom.

In tango one can pull first one foot, then the other so slowly across the wooden floor. It is the way feet caress the world, they are so in love with the music and the ground upon which we are dancing that they must kiss it through the soles of their shoes, first one foot, then the other, as your feet are now kissing the night street where you live.

I want you to drink and drink, my love, all of your winter, all of my summer, all of your darkness full of hot stars turning, all of my sunlight full of cool green falling. Drink them in, and when they are gone, crush the can, our bodies having danced every beat of our liquid hearts away.

LET THE SONG

Let the song of the river go on
its under bed plashing, plunking, rolling
over the river rock smooth
and colored top flow cresting waving dimpling
pulling past to future to past under the
brightly word-drawn bridge...

Let the song of the river go on sing of my mother
in a dress of pearl blue the day I was wed
her white car piled high with gifts tied in silver ribbon
the song bright joy sang as it bumped, choralling on the
sunbursting starlight through the sugar pine trees

Let the moan of the river go on, lush song of sorrow, too, as the
loves tied their black shoes on for one last dance on the
shimmering moving ballroom floor...

Let the river surge and crest fall downhill and fade into creek beds
tinkling away in the undergrowth where the pennyroyal and wild
mint shine with their secret silver light

Let the song of the river go on and let
it muscle past the mighty rump of rock that rises darkly in the
middle and the lesser rocks of red and pink, over olden yellow too,
the bright flicker of fool's gold onto the sandy sand

Let it hide in its silent deepest folds the ring it took from my hand,
gold and graven it was, knowing as it does before I what shall
come to pass...

Let it play hauling forth memory, desire, pity, and the laughter of the little ones, fairy feet dancing in the stone-side grass.

Let the river sing on and on over the folded money and the noise of airplanes unleashed from their beds of steel and the ticker-tape voices of the tin radio, let the river roll over these sounds and let it be triumphant in its crystal flowing laughing tunneling weeping voice

of song…

ABOUT THE AUTHOR

Photo by Sophia Drozd

Doreen Stock is a poet, essayist, and memoir practitioner who has been exploring creative nonfiction for thirty-plus years from the feminine point of view as a wife, mother of three, single human, and grandmother of eleven. Her first book of poems, *The Politics of Splendor*, was part of a New American Writers exhibit at the Frankfurt Book Fair that year. It combined her own poetry and prose poems with her translation from the work of Marina Tsvetaeva and Anna Akhmatova. While raising her three children, she wrote two book-length memoirs: *FIVE: The Transcript of a Journey*, detailing her family's travels through Europe in a VW van, and *My Name is Y*, an anti-nuclear demonstrator's family memoir. She was also a small press (D'Aurora Press) editor and publisher at that time.

The Bookcase, a memoir exploring totalitarianism and the self, was begun in Amsterdam in the eighties, and after that, *Rani*, describing Stock's first five-month stay in Tel Aviv and Jerusalem. During seven years of travel in the nineties, she composed several collections of poems, *Memorial Service, Poems of Arad* among them, and the essays which eventually became *On Leaving Jerusalem: Prose of a Traveling Nature*.

An archive of her reading her work can be found at Marin Poets Live! — YouTube.

COLOPHON

Published in a first edition of 150 soft cover and 50 casebound by Mine Gallery Editions of Fairfax, California.

All typography and text preparation by Wordsworth of San Geronimo, California.

The typeface is Bitstream Charter.

Printed and bound by Ingram Spark in the spring of 2015.

Cover design by Amy Drozd.

CPSIA information can be obtained at www.ICGtesting.com
Printed in the USA
LVIW01n1921230715
447309LV00004B/6